Celebrate Piano! ™

A Comprehensive Piano Method by

Cathy Albergo   J. Mitzi Kolar   Mark Mrozinski

LESSON AND MUSICIANSHIP **1A**

National Library of Canada Cataloguing in Publication Data

Albergo, Cathy, 1951 –
        Celebrate piano : lesson and musicianship / Cathy Albergo, Jane Michelle Kolar,
Mark Mrozinski.

May be used in conjunction with Celebrate piano : solos.
Contents: Level 1A – level 1B – level 2A – level 2B – level 3 – level 4.
ISBN 0-88797-817-7 (level 1A). – ISBN 0-88797-819-3 (level 1B). –
ISBN 0-88797-843-6 (level 2A). – ISBN 0-88797-845-2 (level 2B). –
ISBN 0-88797-857-6 (level 3). – ISBN 0-88797-861-4 (level 4)

        1. Piano–Instruction and study–Juvenile. 2. Piano–Studies and
exercises–Juvenile. 3. Piano music–Teaching pieces–Juvenile. I. Kolar, Jane Michelle
II. Mrozinski, Mark III. Title.

MT746 A328 2002   j786.2'193'076   C2002-902826-4

FREDERICK
HARRIS
MUSIC

Table of Contents

- Steady beat
- LH and RH finger numbers
- 2 and 3 black keys
- Clusters
- Low, middle, and high sounds
- Independent fingers 2, 3
- Braced finger

Music has a steady beat. A ticking clock and your heart also have a steady beat.

Discover the Steady Beat

Listen to the music that your teacher plays.*

➤ Can you feel the beat as you listen?

As you listen to the music:

➤ March and say "ta" to the steady beat.

➤ Tap and say "ta" to the steady beat.

➤ Draw lines to the steady beat.

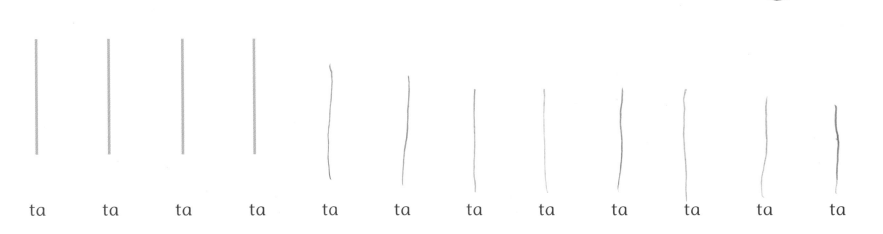

| | | | | | | | | | | | |
ta ta ta ta ta ta ta ta ta ta ta ta

*Teacher: Play the march provided in *Exploring* **Celebrate Piano!**™ or another piece with a steady beat.

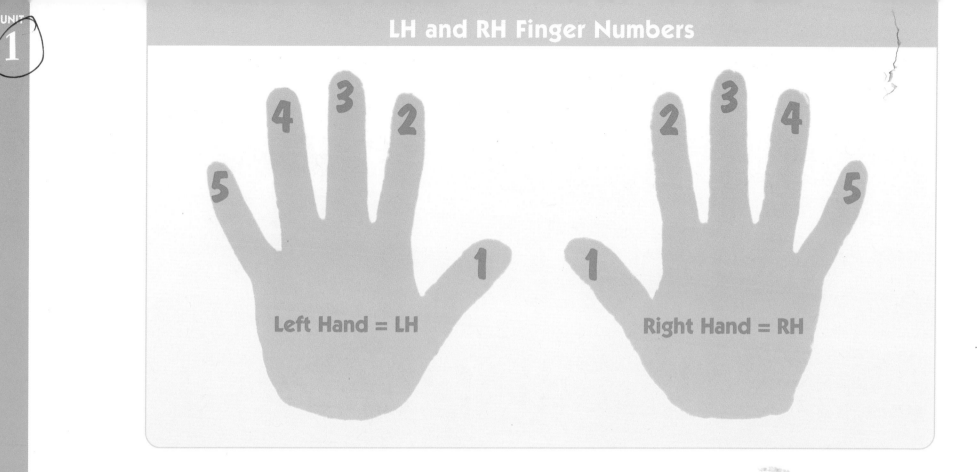

Left Hand = LH

Right Hand = RH

Finger Wiggle Game

Play the Finger Wiggle Game as your teacher or parent calls out the directions. You can use either hand or both hands!

➤ Wiggle finger 2.

➤ Tap your head with finger 5.

➤ Touch your nose with finger 4.

➤ Wiggle finger 1.

➤ Tap your arm with finger 3.

➤ Make up your own finger wiggle games.

Exploring the Keyboard

➤ Circle each group of 2 black keys.

➤ Touch each group of 2 black keys on your keyboard.

➤ With your eyes closed, slide your RH over the black keys.
Find and play the groups of 2 black keys.

➤ Repeat with your LH. Don't peek!

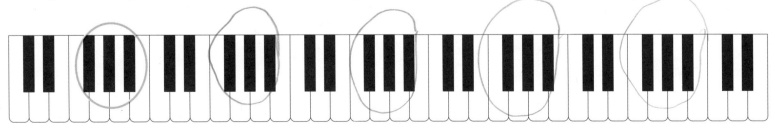

➤ Circle each group of 3 black keys.

➤ Touch each group of 3 black keys on your keyboard.

➤ With your eyes closed, slide your RH over the black keys.
Find and play the groups of 3 black keys.

➤ Repeat with your LH. Remember to keep your eyes closed!

Practice Plan

➤ Tap and say "right, left, right, left..." to the steady beat.

➤ Play and ta each beat. Let each arm drop freely.

➤ Play and sing the words.

Raindrops

Play four times.

Gently

1. Rain - drops,   rain - drops,   hear   the   rain - drops
2. Gen - tly   fall - ing   on   my   win - dow.
3. Rain - drops,   rain - drops,   stead - y   rain - drops;
4. When   they're   o - ver,   see   the   rain - bow.

1-2   1

With accompaniment, student plays:

Teacher accompaniment

mp

con pedale

Practice Plan

➤ Tap and say "left, right, right, right..." to the steady beat.

➤ Play and ta. Play with firm, rounded fingers.

➤ Play and sing the words.

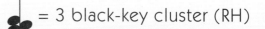
Call of the Drum

Play four times.

With a steady beat

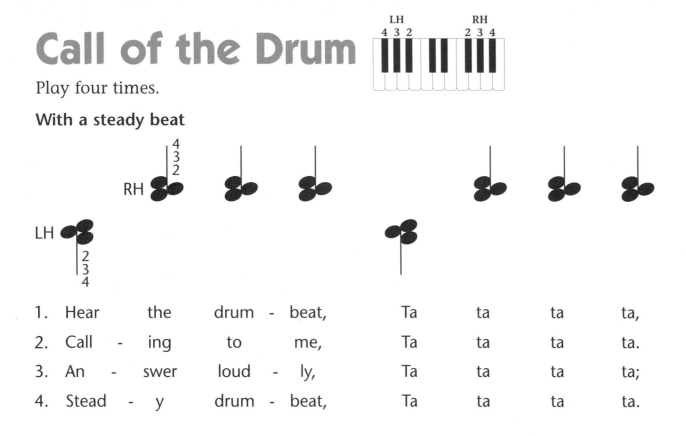

1.	Hear	the	drum - beat,	Ta	ta	ta	ta,
2.	Call -	ing	to	me,	Ta	ta	ta	ta.
3.	An -	swer	loud -	ly,	Ta	ta	ta	ta;
4.	Stead -	y	drum - beat,	Ta	ta	ta	ta.

Student plays:

Teacher accompaniment

3-4   2

Low, Middle, and High Sounds

On the keyboard, low sounds are to the left and high sounds are to the right.

Exploring Sounds

➤ Find and play low, middle, and high sounds on groups of 2 black keys. Listen for the difference in sound.

➤ Find and play low, middle, and high sounds on groups of 3 black keys. Listen for the difference in sound.

On the keyboard below:

➤ Circle in **red** the groups of 2 black keys that sound high.

➤ Circle in **blue** the groups of 3 black keys that sound low.

➤ Draw a box around a group of 2 black keys in the middle of the keyboard.

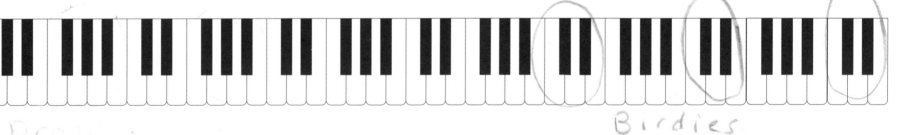

Birdies

Create the Sounds!

➤ What animal makes a low sound? Make the sound of that animal with your voice and on the keyboard.

➤ What animal makes a high sound? Make the sound of that animal with your voice and on the keyboard.

Low, Middle, High Patterns

For each pattern:

➤ Tap and say the hand that plays.

➤ Tap and say "low," "middle," or "high."

➤ Play on the black keys, and say "low," "middle," or "high" as you play.

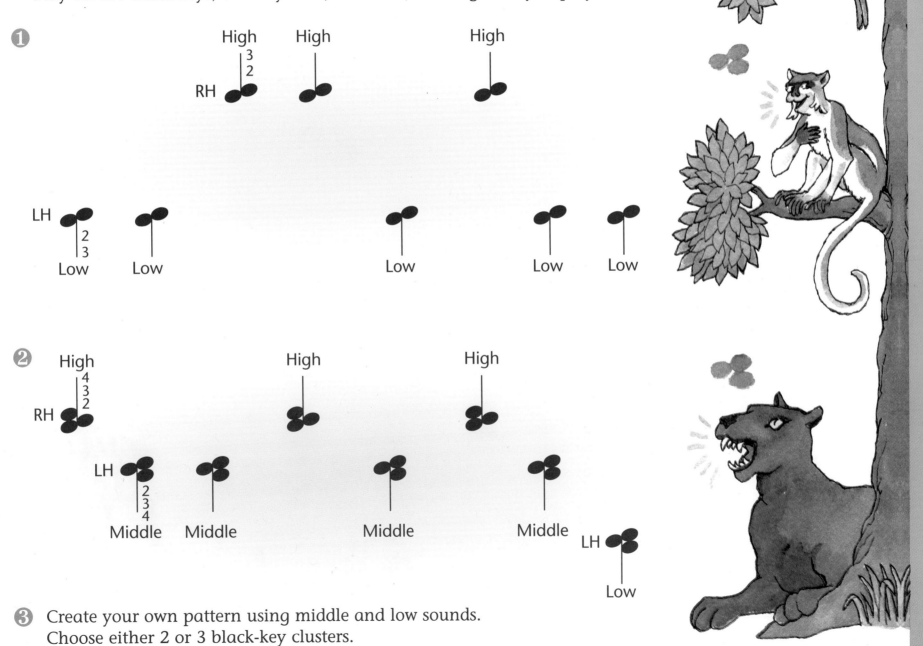

1

High High High
3
2
RH

LH
2
3
Low Low Low Low Low

2 High High High
4
3
2
RH

LH
2
3
4
Middle Middle Middle Middle
LH
Low

3 Create your own pattern using middle and low sounds.
Choose either 2 or 3 black-key clusters.

Cluster Bounce ▲

➤ Play these clusters, moving from low to high and back to low on the keyboard. Bounce the clusters with a relaxed arm drop.

RH
2 3 4

①

RH 4
    3
    2

LH
4 3 2

②

LH 2
    3
    4

③ Make up your own piece using clusters moving from low to high, or high to low.

▲up, down

Finger Number Frolic

➤ Number each finger on these left and right hands.

➤ Play the Finger Wiggle Game on page 4 again.

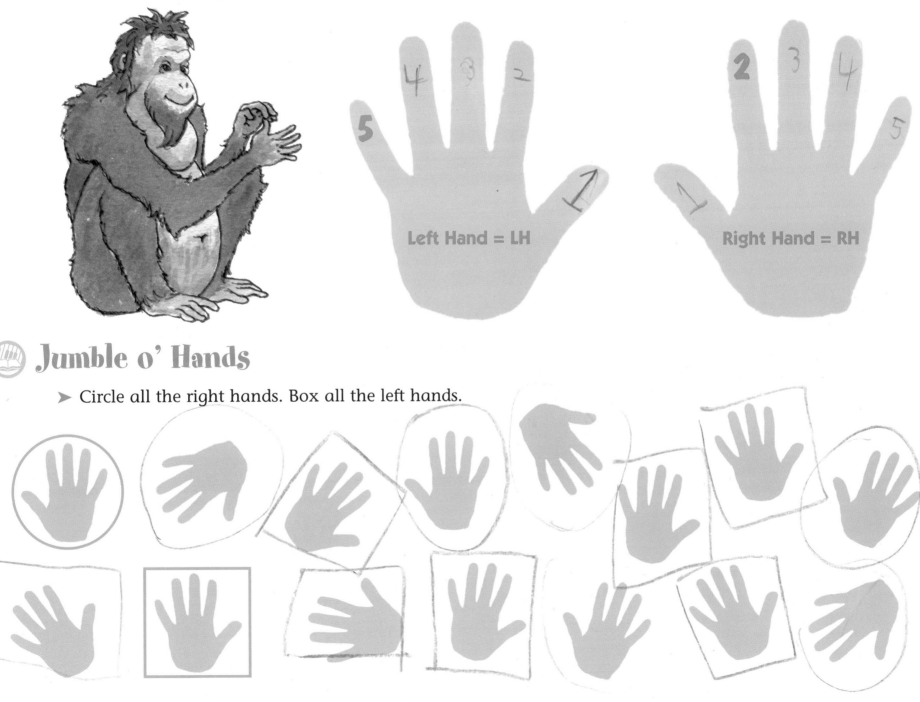

Left Hand = LH

Right Hand = RH

Jumble o' Hands

➤ Circle all the right hands. Box all the left hands.

Black-key Finger Workout ▲

♩ = single note or key

For each example:

➤ Tap and ta with a steady beat.

➤ Say "cluster, cluster, two, three. . ." as you play on the keyboard cover or in the air.

➤ Play and ta. Remember to play with firm, rounded fingers.

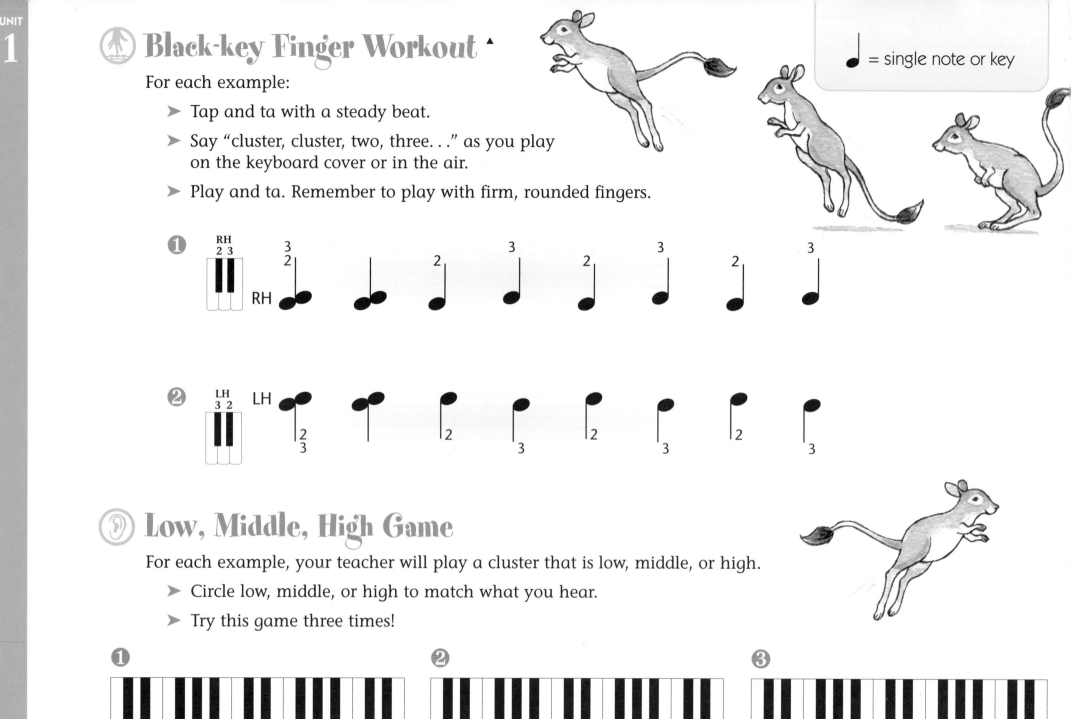

Low, Middle, High Game

For each example, your teacher will play a cluster that is low, middle, or high.

➤ Circle low, middle, or high to match what you hear.

➤ Try this game three times!

❶ Low   Middle   High

❷ Low   Middle   High

❸ Low   Middle   High

▲up, down, same; independent fingers 2, 3

Animal March

➤ What is your favorite animal? Can you imitate its sound?
  Is it high or low? soft or loud?

➤ Make up and play a piece about your favorite animal.

➤ Draw a picture of your favorite animal or a picture of your piece.

p and *f*

The Ants Go Marching

Verse 1 The ants go marching one by one, hurrah, hurrah,
The ants go marching one by one, hurrah, hurrah.
The ants go marching one by one
The last one stops to have some fun
And they all go marching into the earth
To get out of the rain.
Ta, ta, ta, ta, ta, ta, ta, ta.

Verse 2 The ants go marching two by two, hurrah, hurrah,
The ants go marching two by two, hurrah, hurrah.
The ants go marching two by two
The last one stops to tie its shoe
And they all. . .

Verse 3 The ants go marching three by three, hurrah, hurrah,
The ants go marching three by three, hurrah, hurrah.
The ants go marching three by three
The last one stops to climb a tree
And they all. . .

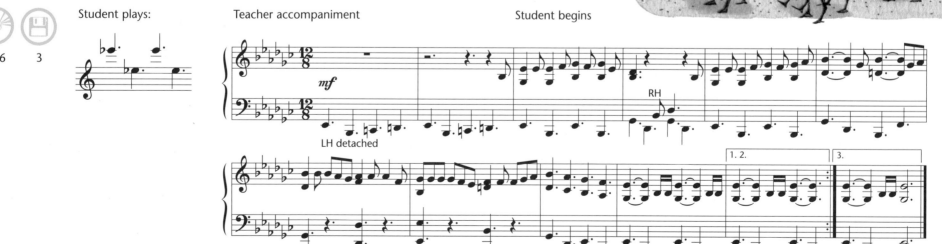

Student plays:

Teacher accompaniment

Student begins

5-6   3

mf

LH detached

RH

Practice Plan

➤ Find your finger position for each verse.
   Play verse 1 with braced finger 3.

➤ Ta and play with a steady beat.
   Let each arm drop freely and play with
   firm, rounded fingers.

➤ Can you sing the words as you play?

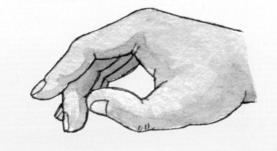

Braced Finger

Support finger 3 with your thumb.

The Ants Go Marching

**Play and sing until
the end of the verse.**

Verse 1

Verse 2

Verse 3

UNIT 2

- Rhythm: ♩ and ♪
- Up, down, and same
- Independent fingers 2, 3, 4
- Transpose

Rhythm is a pattern of short and long sounds.

Quarter note ♩ = short sound = ta   Half note ♪ = long sound = ta-ah

Clap quarter notes and say: Clap half notes and say:

short	short	short	short
ta	ta	ta	ta

lo - ong	lo - ong
ta - ah	ta - ah

Ⓕ Clapping Patterns

F1

➤ Clap and say this rhythmic pattern with a steady beat:

short	short	lo - ong	short	short	lo - ong	lo - ong	lo - ong	short	short	lo - ong
ta	ta	ta - ah	ta	ta	ta - ah	ta - ah	ta - ah	ta	ta	ta - ah

Rhythm Warm-ups

➤ Point to the notes and say "ta" or "ta-ah."

➤ Play in your lap and say which hand plays.

➤ Play and ta with a steady beat. Remember to play with firm, rounded fingers.

Practice Plan

➤ Point to the notes and say "ta" or "ta-ah."

➤ Tap and say "right, right, le-eft..."

➤ Play with a steady beat and say "ta" or "ta-ah." Remember to use a relaxed arm drop.

➤ Play and sing the words.

Swinging Monkeys

Play twice.

Playfully

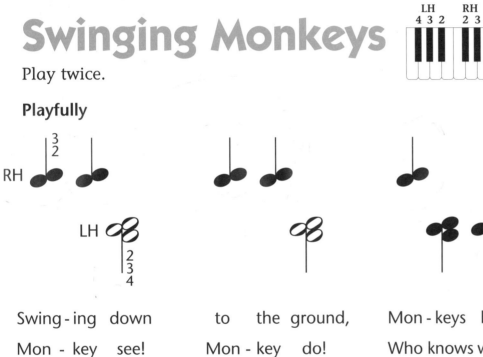

Swing - ing down   to   the ground,   Mon - keys love   to   play   a - round.
Mon - key   see!   Mon - key do!   Who knows what those mon - keys   do!

Student plays: Teacher accompaniment

11-12   6

Up, Down, and Same

Notes can:

go up

go down

stay the same

On the keyboard:

sounds going up move to the right

sounds going down move to the left

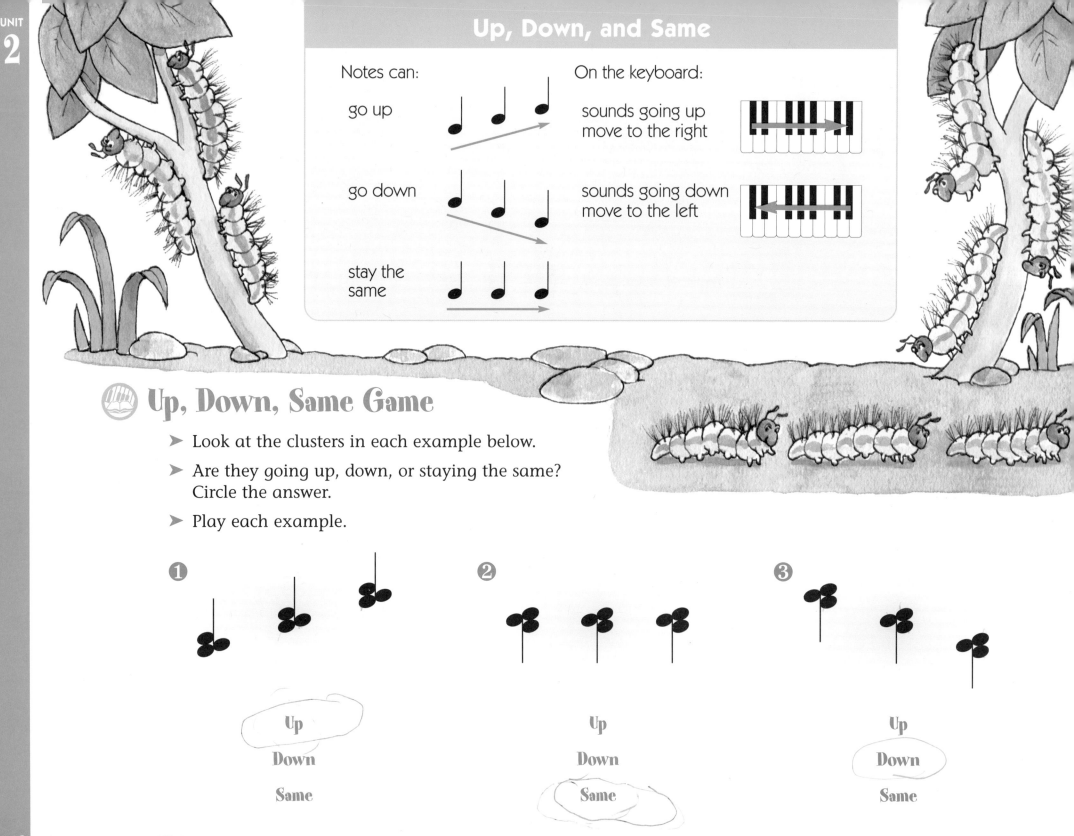

Up, Down, Same Game

➤ Look at the clusters in each example below.

➤ Are they going up, down, or staying the same? Circle the answer.

➤ Play each example.

❶

Up

Down

Same

❷

Up

Down

Same

❸

Up

Down

Same

Middle C Safari

A safari is an exciting journey.
Your teacher will help you find Middle C on the keyboard.

➤ Play the **Middle C Song** with any finger and sing:
"This is the sound of Mid-dle C."
Match your voice with the sound of Middle C.

➤ Sing Middle C every time you pass the piano.

➤ Play Middle C to check if your voice matches.

Connect the Hands

➤ Draw a line to connect all the right hands
from start to finish.

START

FINISH

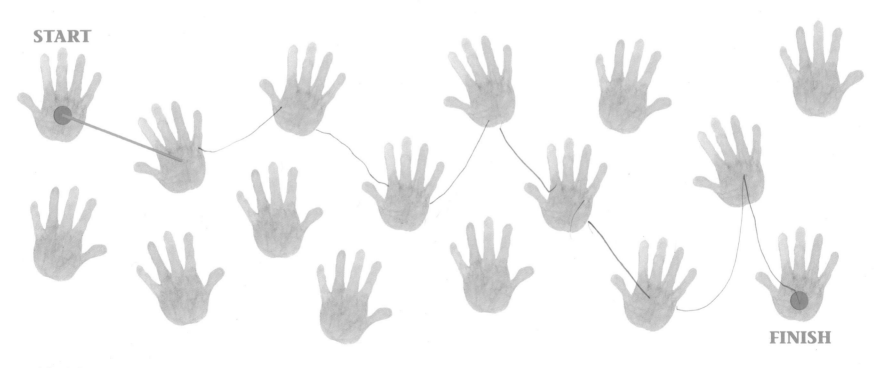

*Middle C Song

This   is the sound of   Mid - dle   C.

Practice Plan

➤ Point to the notes and ta with a steady beat.

➤ Tap and say which hand plays.

➤ Play and ta using a braced finger 2 in each hand.

➤ Play and say the words.

Going Up and Down

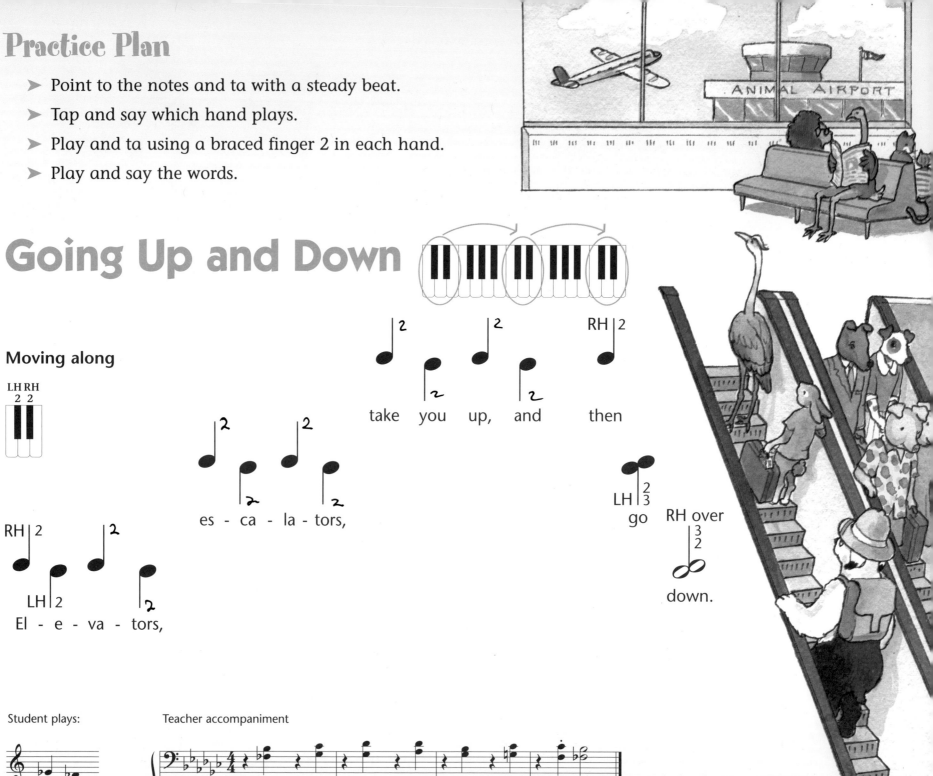

Moving along

LH RH
2 2

take you up, and then

RH 2

LH 2
go   RH over

es - ca - la - tors,

LH 2 3
3 2
down.

RH 2

LH 2
El - e - va - tors,

13-14   7

Student plays:

Teacher accompaniment

mf

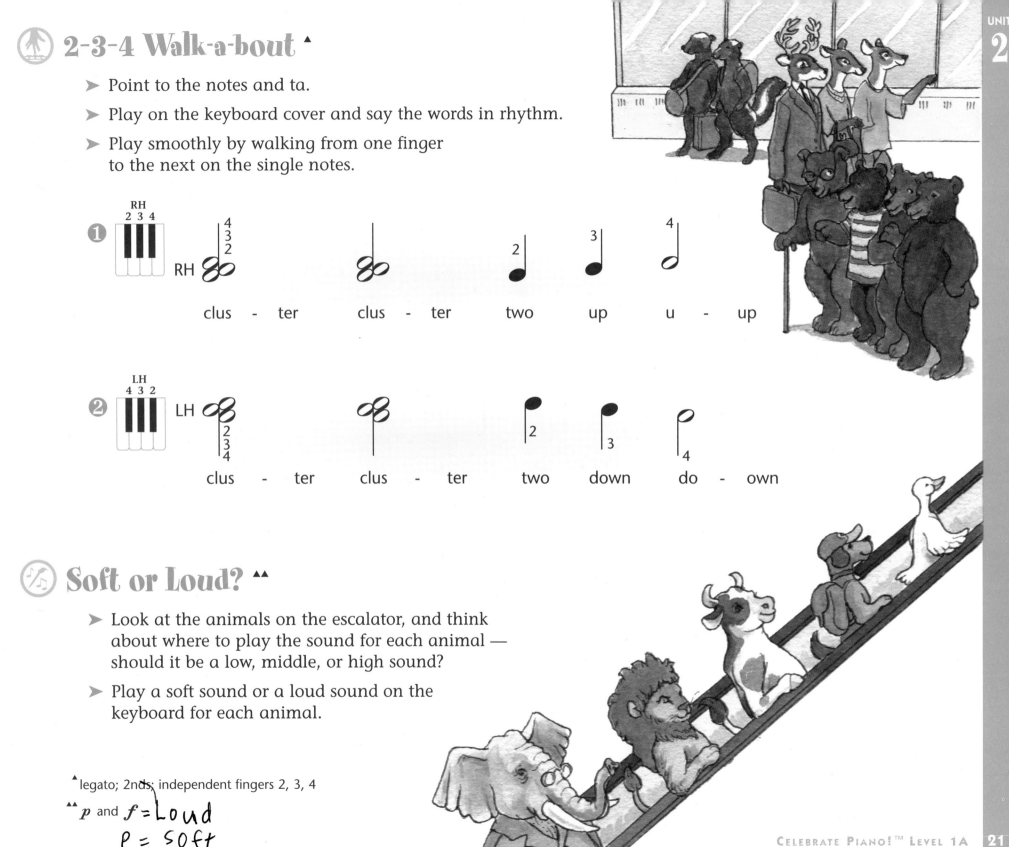

2-3-4 Walk-a-bout ▲

➤ Point to the notes and ta.

➤ Play on the keyboard cover and say the words in rhythm.

➤ Play smoothly by walking from one finger to the next on the single notes.

① RH

clus – ter   clus – ter   two   up   u – up

② LH

clus – ter   clus – ter   two   down   do – own

Soft or Loud? ▲▲

➤ Look at the animals on the escalator, and think about where to play the sound for each animal — should it be a low, middle, or high sound?

➤ Play a soft sound or a loud sound on the keyboard for each animal.

▲legato; 2nds; independent fingers 2, 3, 4

▲▲ *p* and *f* = Loud
p = soft

Practice Plan

➤ Point to the notes and ta with a steady beat.

➤ Tap and say which hand plays. Is the RH always the same?

➤ Practice the hand moves.

➤ Play and ta. Walk smoothly between the single notes.

Rocket Ships

Steadily

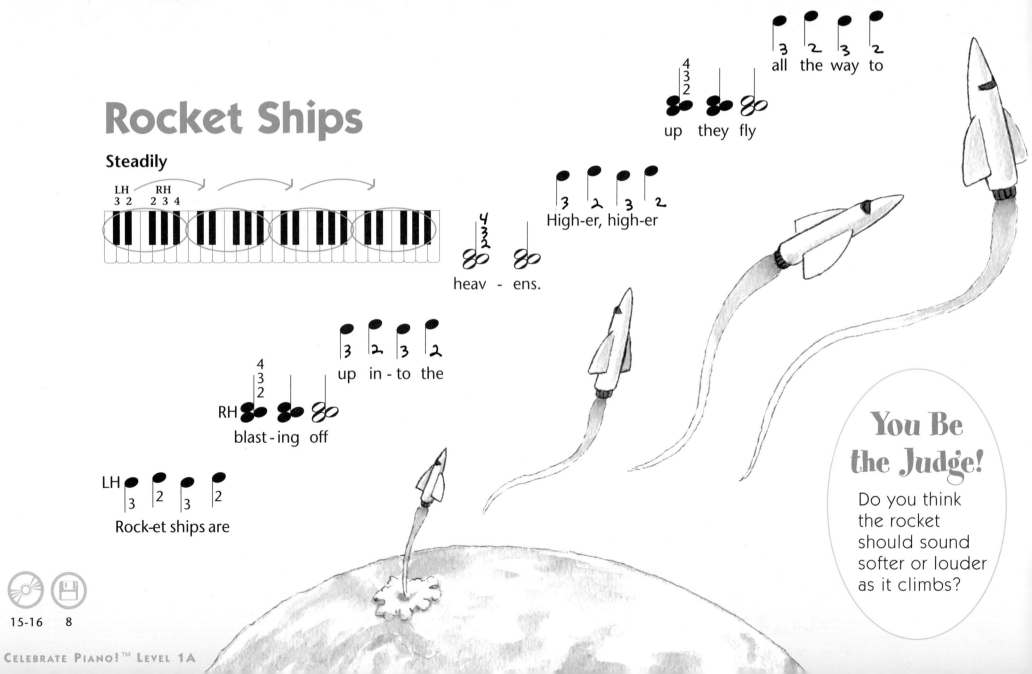

Sat - urn!

all the way to

up they fly

High-er, high-er

heav - ens.

up in - to the

blast - ing off

Rock-et ships are

You Be the Judge!

Do you think the rocket should sound softer or louder as it climbs?

Practice Plan

➤ Point to the notes and ta with a steady beat.

➤ Tap and say which hand plays. Practice the hand moves.

➤ Play and ta.

➤ Play softly the first time and loudly the second time.

Transpose

UNIT 2

Transpose means to play the same piece in a new position on the keyboard.

Boogie Down

Play twice.

Dancing

Go down, boog - ie down,
Swing - ing to the sound,

Danc - ing round and round.
Go down, boog - ie down.

Transpose

Play **Boogie Down** in this new position:

Student plays:

Teacher accompaniment

17-18   9

🎧 Hide and Seek Patterns

Listen as your teacher plays one of the rhythmic patterns in each example.

➤ Circle the rhythm that you hear.

❶

❷

❸

🎧 Echo Game—Clapbacks!

Listen as your teacher claps a pattern.

➤ Imitate your teacher by clapping the same pattern.

🎧 Echo Game—Playbacks! ▲

Listen as your teacher plays a pattern on the 3 black keys.

➤ Sing the pattern your teacher plays.

➤ Play the pattern on the 3 black keys.

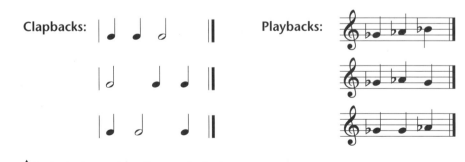

Clapbacks: Playbacks:

▲ 2nds; independent fingers 2, 3, 4

The Elephant and the Mouse ▲

Make up a musical story about an elephant and a mouse.
Play it on white or black keys.

➤ Choose from: up, down, same
                soft, loud
                ta, ta-ah

➤ Write or draw your piece using single notes, clusters, wavy lines, or anything you like.

mouse

twinkle A - high
Bread only

Elephant

Twinkle A - Low
Bread, Peanut Butter,
Jelly, Bread

p and *f*

Practice Plan

Write your own Practice Plan.

➤ Sticker for each practice!
➤ Practice every day !
➤ Play nice!
➤ Have fun !

Hot Cross Buns

Play twice.

Folk song

1. Hot cross buns,   hot cross buns,   one and two and hot cross buns.
2. Hot cross buns,   hot cross buns,   who will buy my hot cross buns?

19-20   10

Student plays: Teacher accompaniment

- The music staff:
  Line notes and space notes
- Interval: 2nd or step
- Dynamics: p and f
- Phrase
- Independent fingers 1, 2, 3

Left–Right–Both Workout!

LH   RH
2   2 3

➤ Point and ta with a steady beat.

➤ Tap and say which hand plays (left, right, or both).

➤ Play and ta.

Middle C Safari

➤ Play the **Middle C Song** with any finger and sing:
  "This is the sound of Mid-dle C."

➤ Match your voice with the sound of Middle C.

➤ Sing Middle C every time you pass the piano.

➤ Play Middle C to check if your voice matches.

▲ HT; 2nds

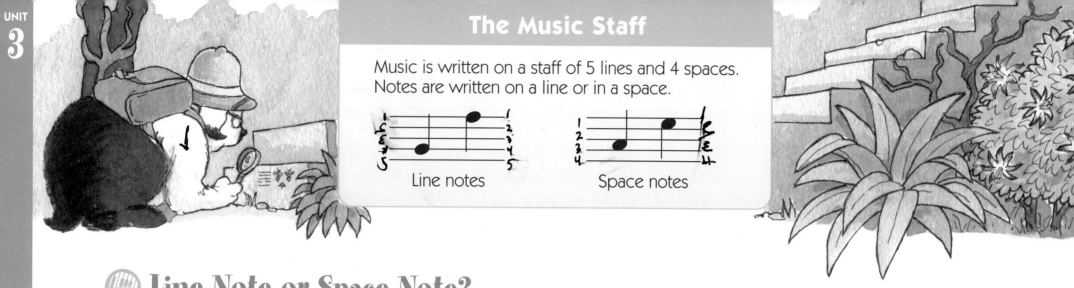

The Music Staff

Music is written on a staff of 5 lines and 4 spaces.
Notes are written on a line or in a space.

Line notes   Space notes

Line Note or Space Note?

➤ Identify each note on the staff below. Write **L** for Line note or **S** for Space note.

L   S   S   L   S   L   L

Drawing Notes

➤ Draw a space note (S) or line note (L) on the staff as shown. You may draw ♩ or ♪.

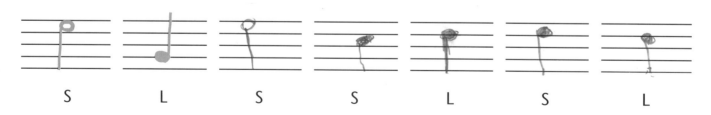

S   L   S   S   L   S   L

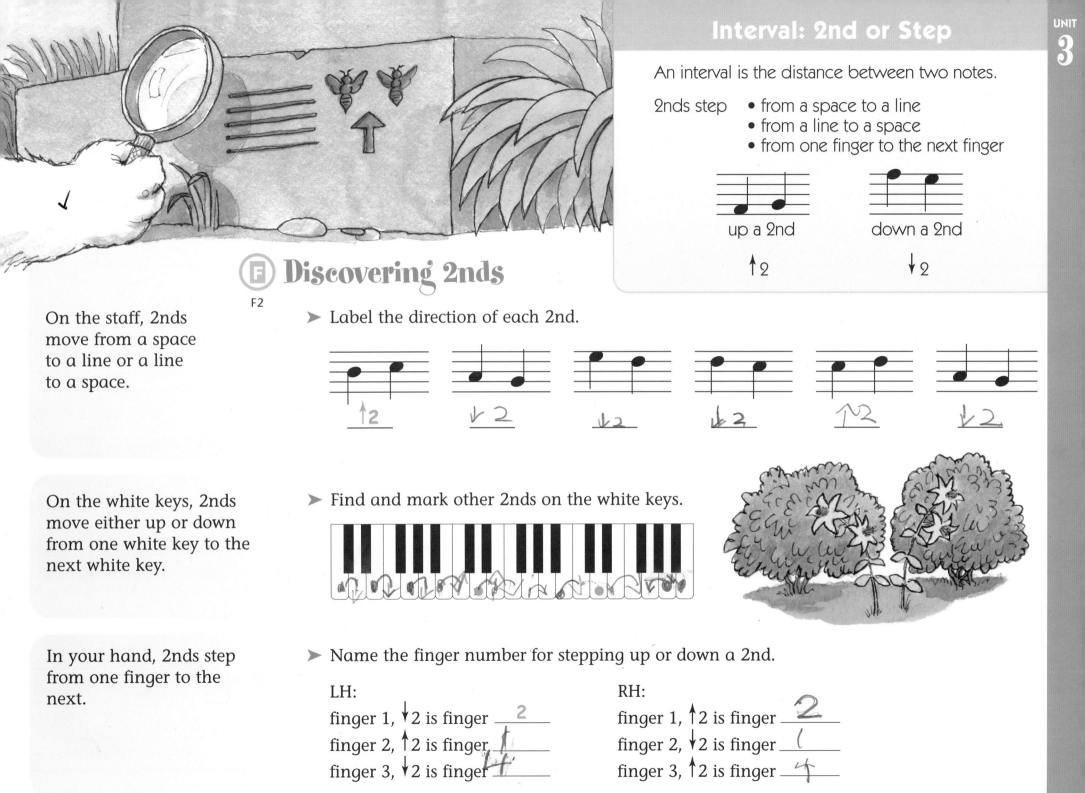

An interval is the distance between two notes.

2nds step
• from a space to a line
• from a line to a space
• from one finger to the next finger

up a 2nd   down a 2nd

↑2   ↓2

Ⓕ Discovering 2nds

F2

On the staff, 2nds move from a space to a line or a line to a space.

➤ Label the direction of each 2nd.

↑2   ↓2   ↓2   ↓3   ↑2   ↓2

On the white keys, 2nds move either up or down from one white key to the next white key.

➤ Find and mark other 2nds on the white keys.

In your hand, 2nds step from one finger to the next.

➤ Name the finger number for stepping up or down a 2nd.

LH:
finger 1, ↓2 is finger __2__
finger 2, ↑2 is finger __1__
finger 3, ↓2 is finger __4__

RH:
finger 1, ↑2 is finger __2__
finger 2, ↓2 is finger __1__
finger 3, ↑2 is finger __4__

Stepping Along

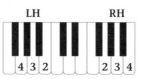

➤ Tap and ta the rhythm.

➤ Say the interval direction and size.

➤ Say the finger numbers as you play.

❶ RH

Say: start ↑2 ↓2 ↑2 ↑2 ↓2 ↓2

❷ LH

Say: start same ↑2 ↓2 ↓2 same

Practice Plan

➤ **T** = Tap and ta the rhythm with a steady beat.

➤ Say the interval direction and size. (Start, up a 2nd...)

➤ Play and ta.

➤ Play and sing the words. End each line softly.

Deep Blue Sea

Calmly

RH
2 3 2 3 4 3 2   3 4 3 4 3 3

Swim-ming in the deep blue sea,   dol-phins, whales and sword-fish.

Say: start ↑2 ↓2 ↑2 ↑2 ↓2 ↓2

LH 4 3 4 3 2 3 4   3 3 2 3 4 4

Liv - ing in the deep blue sea,   clams and shrimp and star-fish.

start ↑2 ↓2

Transpose

Play **Deep Blue Sea** in this new position:

LH 4 3 2   RH 2 3 4

Student plays:

Teacher accompaniment

25-26   13

mp

Practice Plan

➤ **T** = Tap and ta the rhythm with a steady beat.

➤ Tap and say which hand plays.

➤ Say the interval direction and size.

➤ Play and ta or sing the words.

Dynamics tell you how softly or loudly to play. *Piano* and *forte* are called dynamics.

Piano is the Italian word for soft.

Forte is the Italian word for loud.

p = play softly

f = play loudly

Whisper or Shout

Steadily

Whis-per soft - ly   in   my   ear,   Shout   loud - ly   when   you   cheer!

start ↑2 ↑2 ↓2   start ↓2 same

You Be the Judge!

Did you hear:
- a steady beat?
- ***p*** and ***f*** ?

27-28   14

Student plays:

Teacher accompaniment

Practice Plan

➤ **T** = Tap and ta the rhythm with a steady beat.

➤ Tap and say which hand plays.

➤ Say the interval direction and size.

➤ Play and ta.

➤ Play and sing the words.

Brass Band

Play twice.

Marching

Brass band march-ing, here they come, Tu - bas, trum-pets, big bass drum!
See them march-ing, hear them play, Cel - e - brate this spe - cial day!

Transpose

Play **Brass Band** on these white keys:

Student plays:

Teacher accompaniment

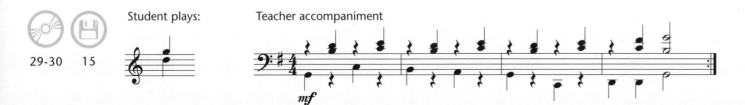

29-30   15

Practice Plan

➤ **T** = Tap and ta.

➤ Tap and say which hand plays.

➤ **I** = Say the interval direction and size.

➤ Play and ta. Remember to play smoothly and end the phrases softly.

➤ How many phrases can you find? 4

A phrase is a group of notes. A phrase mark is a curved line over the phrase. Play the notes within the phrase mark smoothly. At the end of the phrase, play the last note softly and lift your hand.

Clouds

Drifting

p See the clouds go drift-ing by, Way up in the blue sky.

Shapes and forms of man-y things, What can you i-mag-ine?

Transpose

Play **Clouds** on these black keys:

Student plays:

Teacher accompaniment

p con pedale

31-32 16

Fun Thumb Phrases! ▲

LH   RH

3 2 1 1 2

➤ Point and ta with a steady beat.

➤ Play on the keyboard cover and say which hand plays.

➤ Say the interval direction and size.

➤ Play smoothly. At the end of each phrase, play the last note softly and lift your hand.

RH
1   2   1   2   1

LH 3   2   1

p

2nd Chance

➤ Write a 2nd up or down from the given note.

↑2   ↑2   ↓2   ↑2   ↑2   ↓2

Alphabet Cheer! ▲▲

➤ Echo your teacher's cheer.

➤ Can you cheer backwards? G, F, E, D, C, B, A!

Cheers:

A B C D E F G

G F E D C B A

A B C D E F G

▲ legato; independent fingers 1, 2, 3

▲▲ music alphabet

Transpose

Play **Fun Thumb Phrases!** on these white keys:

LH   RH

3 2 1 1 2

Rhythm Taps

➤ Tap and ta each rhythm line.

➤ Play and ta each rhythm line on any black key.

➤ Using one of these rhythm lines, create your own song on the black keys.

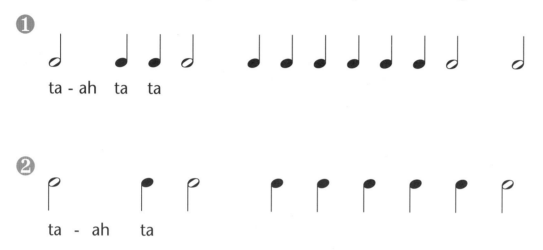

❶

ta - ah   ta   ta

❷

ta - ah   ta

Interval Safari: Busy Bee Song

The **Busy Bee Song** uses 2nds.

➤ Sing and play the **Busy Bee Song**. Start on Middle C with RH finger 2.

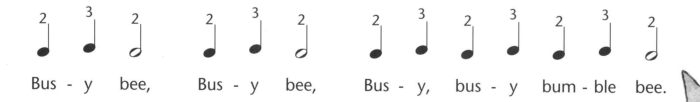

Bus - y   bee,   Bus - y   bee,   Bus - y,   bus - y   bum - ble   bee.

➤ Sing this new song at least twice a day, playing only to check that your voice matches the piano sound.

🎧 Game o' Listening

Listen as your teacher plays one of the rhythmic patterns in each example.

➤ Circle the rhythm that you hear.

①

②

③

👂 Echo Game–Clapbacks! ▲

Listen as your teacher claps a pattern.

➤ Imitate your teacher by clapping the same pattern.

🎧 Echo Game–Playbacks! ▲

Listen as your teacher plays a pattern on the 2 black keys.

➤ Sing the pattern your teacher plays.

➤ Play the pattern on the 2 black keys.

Clapbacks:

Playbacks:

My Day at the Circus

Create your own song on the black keys.

➤ Choose from: *p* and *f*

high, middle, low sounds

♩ and ♪

➤ Draw your song in any way you like!

Julianne's
Day at the Circus

I went to the circus.
4   3   2   3   4 2

I Bought some popcorn.
4   1   3   4   2

I Bought some candy.
4   2   3   4 2

I Bought some drinks.
4   2   3   4 2

I had a fun, fun day!
4   2   3   4   4   2

♩ ♩ ♩
2 3 4

Pop corn

Practice Plan

➤ **T** = Tap and ta.

➤ Tap and say which hand plays.

➤ How many phrases can you find?
Remember to end the phrases softly.

➤ Play and ta or sing the words.

Prairie Song

Not too fast

Lis - ten   to   the   cold   wind   blow   through   the   mead - ow   grass   –   es.

Our   log   cab - in   keeps   us   warm   un - til   the   win - ter   pass   –   es.

You Be the Judge!

Did you hear:
- smooth phrases?
- *p*?

Student plays:

Teacher accompaniment

33-34   17

- Measure and bar line
- Legato
- Melodic and harmonic 2nds
- Repeated patterns
- The music alphabet
- Letter clefs
- The CDE group
- Hands together

Two Staffs

Music for both hands often uses 2 staffs:
- the top staff is usually for RH
- the bottom staff is usually for LH

Two-staff Stepping ▲

➤ Tap and ta the exercise.

➤ Say the interval direction and size.

➤ Say the finger numbers and play on the keyboard cover.

➤ Play. Remember the phrase marks and play smoothly.

LH   RH

3 2 1   1 2 3

Middle C

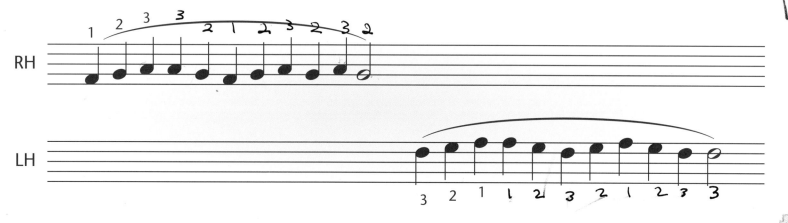

RH

LH

Interval Safari

➤ Sing the **Middle C Song**. Play Middle C on the keyboard to check that your voice matches Middle C.

➤ Sing the **Busy Bee Song** (2nds). Play Middle C and D (up a 2nd) to check that you are singing in tune.

▲legato

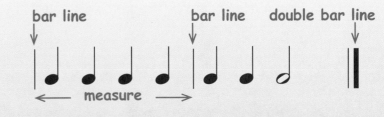

Bar lines divide the music into groups of beats called measures. The double bar line shows the end of the piece.

bar line   bar line   double bar line

measure

F Bar Line Search

F3

➤ Tap and ta each rhythmic pattern.

1

ta   ta   ta   ta   ta-ah   ta-ah   ta-ah   ta   ta   ta   ta   ta-ah

➤ How many bar lines can you find? __4__

➤ How many measures are in this example? __4__

➤ Circle the double bar line.

2

ta-ah   ta   ta-ah   ta   ta   ta   ta   ta   ta-ah

➤ How many bar lines can you find? __4__

➤ How many measures are in this example? __4__

➤ Circle the double bar line.

Practice Plan

➤ **T** = Tap and ta.

➤ **I** = Say the interval direction and size.

➤ How many phrases are there?
Remember to play legato.

➤ Play and ta or sing the words.

Lullaby

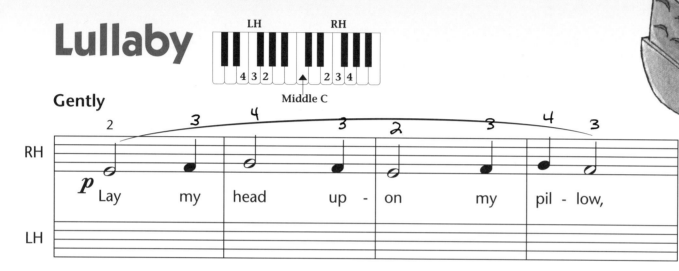

Gently

Lay   my   head   up - on   my   pil - low,

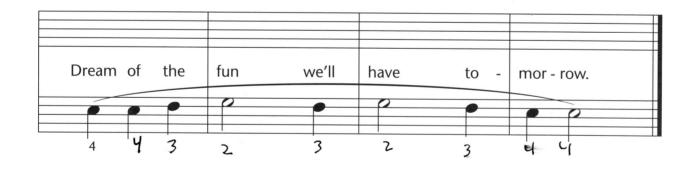

Dream of the fun we'll have to - mor - row.

Transpose

Play **Lullaby** in this new position:

Middle C

39-40   20

Student plays:

Teacher accompaniment

p con pedale

Melodic and Harmonic 2nds

Melodic 2nd:
A melodic 2nd has single notes played one at a time.

Harmonic 2nd:
A harmonic 2nd has two notes played together.

Wait ... A Second!

F

F4

➤ Circle the correct answer: melodic 2nd or harmonic 2nd.

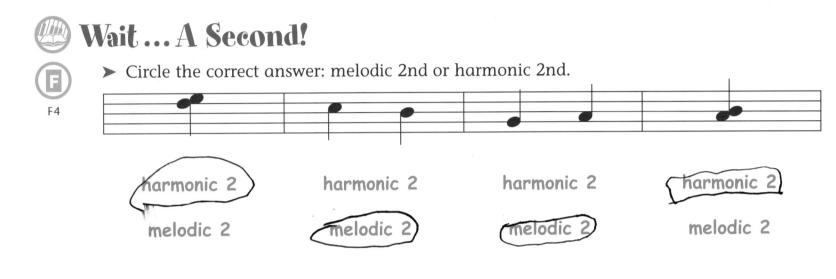

harmonic 2

melodic 2

harmonic 2

melodic 2

harmonic 2

melodic 2

harmonic 2

melodic 2

➤ Write a melodic 2nd or a harmonic 2nd above or below the given note on the staff.

↑melodic 2   ↑harmonic 2   ↓melodic 2   ↓harmonic 2

Repeated Patterns

A group of notes can form a pattern.
Patterns may be repeated.

Pattern Search

➤ Find and circle the
repeated pattern
in the LH.

➤ Play and ta.

Practice Plan

➤ **T** = _tap and ta_

➤ **I** = Say the interval direction and size.

➤ Which hand plays melodic 2nds? _Right_ harmonic 2nds? _Left_

➤ Find and circle another pattern like the circled pattern.

➤ Play and ta.

Busy Bee Toccata

Buzzing busily

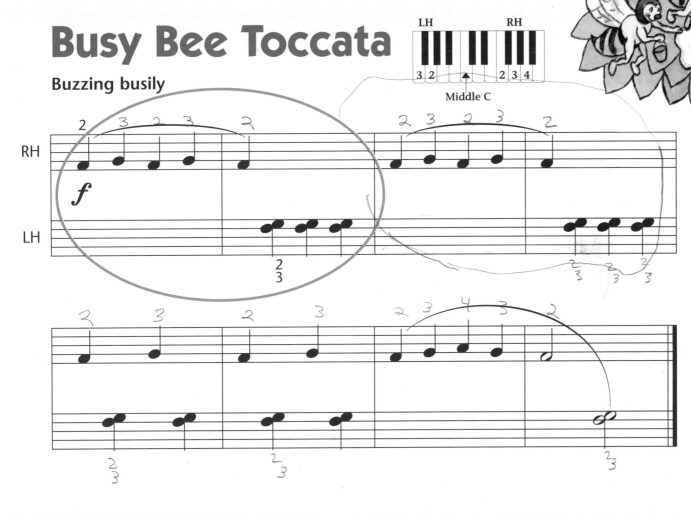

Student plays:

Teacher accompaniment

41-42   21

The Music Alphabet — A B C D E F G

The first seven letters of the alphabet name the white keys.

A B C D E F G A B C D E F G

Naming the White Keys

➤ Play and name all the white keys from lowest to highest on your keyboard. Use either hand.

➤ Write in the missing letters on the white keys.

F G A B C D E F G A B C D E F G A B C D E F G A B C D E F G A B

Alphabet Speller

➤ Fill in the missing music alphabet letters.

1. A __B__ __C__ __D__ __E__ __F__ G

2. E __F__ __G__ __A__ __B__ __C__ D

3. C __D__ __E__ __F__ __G__ __A__ B

4. F __G__ __A__ __B__ __C__ __D__ E

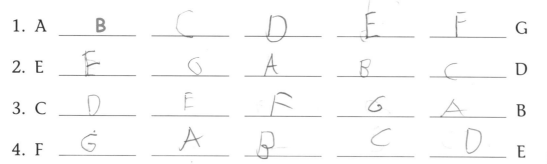

Practice Plan

➤ **T** = _tap and ta_

➤ **I** = Say the interval direction and size.

➤ Circle the letter clef.

➤ Play the entire piece with RH braced finger 2 as you ta. Repeat with the LH.

➤ Play and sing the names of the notes.

Letter Clefs

A letter at the beginning of each staff tells you the name of the starting note.

A →

Stem Direction

When notes are written on a staff, the stems may go up or down for either hand.

Alphabet Song

Start on any A.

With a steady beat

A → *f* A   B   C   D   E   F   G   G   F   E   D   C   B   A

A → Walk-ing   up   the   al-pha-bet.   Let's   go   down and   don't   for-get!

43-44   22   Student plays: Teacher accompaniment

📖 Alphabet Hunt

➤ How many CDE groups can you find on your keyboard?

➤ Play all the CDE groups from low to high. Use fingers 2–3–4.

➤ Circle the CDE groups and write the letters on the keyboard below.

🌳 Phrase the Legato ▲

➤ Tap and ta each exercise on the CDE group.

➤ Sing the finger numbers as you play on the keyboard cover.

➤ Play legato and end the phrase softly.

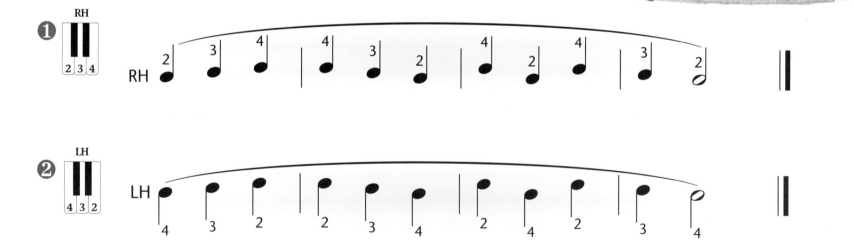

▲3rds; fingers 2–4

Practice Plan

➤ **T I** = _tap, interval direction & size_
➤ Sing the finger numbers as you play on the keyboard cover.
➤ **P** = Phrases and patterns. How many phrases are there?
➤ Name the starting note for each hand.
➤ Play and ta or sing the note names.

Waltz
A waltz is a graceful dance with three beats in each measure.

CDE Waltz

LH   RH
4 3 2   2 3 4
Middle C

Gracefully

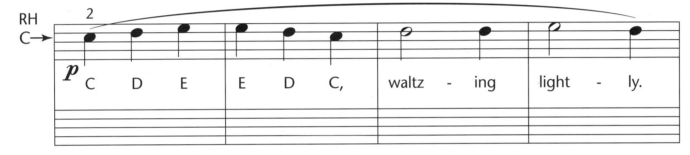

RH
C →
p C   D   E   E   D   C,   waltz - ing   light - ly.

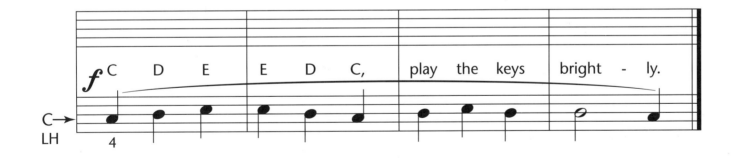

f C   D   E   E   D   C,   play the keys   bright - ly.
C →
LH

You Be the Judge!

Did you hear:
- a steady beat?
- *p* and *f*?
- two phrases?

45-46   23

Student plays:

Teacher accompaniment

Practice Plan

➤ **T I** = _tap, interval + size_

➤ Which hand starts? _R H_

➤ **P** = Phrases and patterns. How many phrases are there? _4_

➤ Find and circle the repeated pattern.

➤ Play and sing the note names, or the words.

Scooter

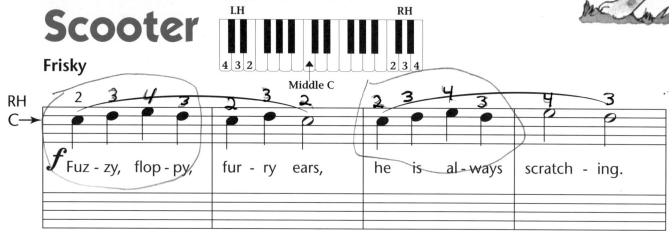

Frisky

RH
C→

2 3 4 3 | 2 3 2 | 2 3 4 3 | 4 3

f Fuz - zy, flop - py, | fur - ry ears, | he is al - ways | scratch - ing.

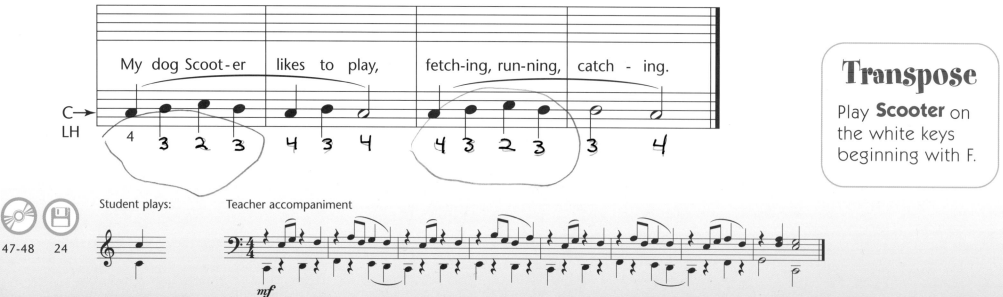

My dog Scoot-er | likes to play, | fetch-ing, run-ning, | catch - ing.

C→
LH

4 3 2 3 | 4 3 4 | 4 3 2 3 | 3 4

Transpose

Play **Scooter** on the white keys beginning with F.

Student plays: Teacher accompaniment

47-48   24

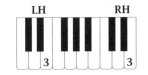

Hands Together Challenge

➤ Say which hand plays.

➤ Play and ta. Use braced finger 3 in each hand.

When notes appear on both staffs, one above the other, play hands together.

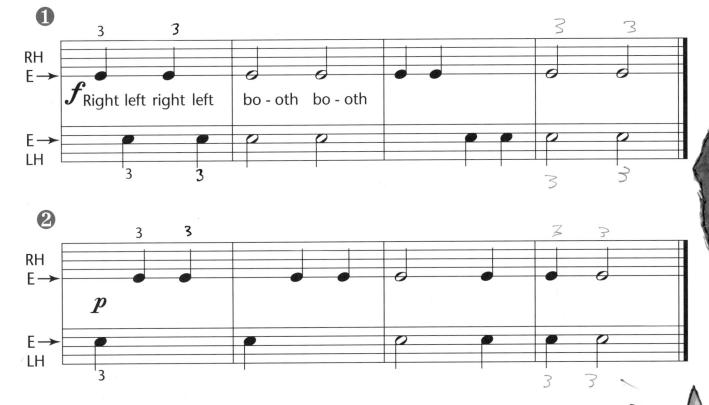

Bar Line Discovery

➤ Place a ✔ above each bar line. Draw an ✖ over the double bar line.

➤ How many measures are there in this example? 4

➤ Tap and ta the rhythm line.

➤ Play on any black key, using a braced finger 2.

Follow the 2nd

➤ Start on the white key marked with a ✔, then follow the directions.

➤ Put an ✖ on the white key where you finish, and name it.

❶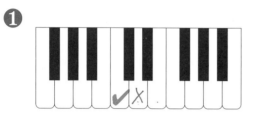

Start, go up a 2nd,
up a 2nd, down a 2nd.

_____D_____

❷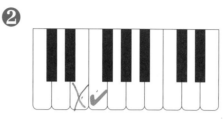

Start, go down a 2nd,
up a 2nd, down a 2nd.

_____E_____

❸

Start, go up a 2nd, up a
2nd, up a 2nd, down a 2nd.

_____G_____

Reading Rhythms

➤ Clap and ta each example. ✔

➤ Play on any key with braced finger 2 as you ta.

➤ Create your own song, using one of the rhythm lines.
Use 2nds going up and down.

❶ RH

❷ LH

❸ LH

👂 What Do You Hear?

Listen as your teacher plays one of the 2nds in each example.

➤ Is it a melodic 2nd or a harmonic 2nd? Circle what you hear.

① melodic   harmonic   **②** melodic   harmonic   **③** melodic   harmonic

👂 Echo Game–Clapbacks! ▲

Listen as your teacher claps a short rhythmic pattern.

➤ Echo or clap what you hear!

Copy Cat

👂 Echo Game–Playbacks! ▲▲

Listen as your teacher plays a melodic pattern.

➤ Sing the pattern that you hear.

➤ Play the pattern in this position:

RH
1 2 3 4

Clapbacks: Playbacks:

▲ 𝅘𝅥𝅭 and 𝅝   ▲▲ FGAB; independent fingers 1, 2, 3, 4

🎵 Mountain Climbing

Make up your own piece about **Mountain Climbing**.

➤ Choose from: CDE

  ~~melodic 2nds~~

  harmonic 2nds

  p or *f*

➤ Write or draw your song using any symbols that you wish.

Practice Plan

➤ **T I** = ___tap 1-interval___

➤ Say the finger numbers as you play on the keyboard cover.

➤ **P** = Phrases. How many phrases are there?

➤ What is the name of the last note?

➤ Find and circle the repeated patterns.

Merrily We Roll Along

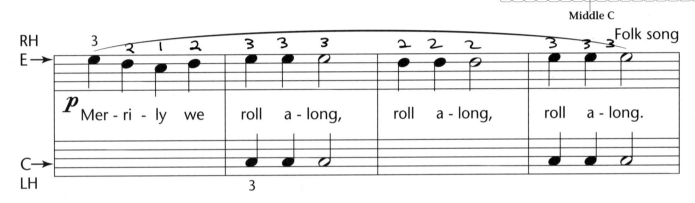

LH   RH

Middle C

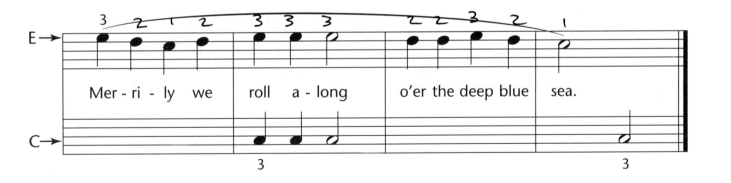

Folk song

RH
E →
3 2 1 2 3 3 3 2 2 2 3 3 3

p Mer - ri - ly we | roll a - long, | roll a - long, | roll a - long.

C →
LH
3

E →
3 2 1 2 3 3 3 2 2 3 2 1

Mer - ri - ly we | roll a - long | o'er the deep blue | sea.

C →
3   3

Transpose

Play **Merrily We Roll Along** on the 3 black-key group.

49-50   25

Student plays:

Teacher accompaniment

p

- Independent fingers 1, 2, 3, 4
- The FGAB group
- Interval: 3rd or skip
- Repeat sign
- Melodic and harmonic 3rds

Finger Aerobics ▲

➤ Warm up your fingers by playing each exercise.

➤ Play legato with firm, rounded fingers.

➤ Play again using short, detached sounds.

❶

RH | 4 3 | 2 1 | 2 3 | 1 ‖

❷

LH | 1 2 | 3 4 | 3 2 | 4 ‖

Interval Safari

➤ Sing the **Middle C Song**.
Check that your voice matches Middle C.   Page 19

➤ Sing the **Busy Bee Song** (2nds). Play
Middle C and D (up a 2nd) to check   36
that you are singing in tune.

Teacher: Have your student identify harmonic and melodic 2nds.

▲3rds; staccato; independent fingers 1, 2, 3, 4

The FGAB Group

The FGAB group is in front of the group of 3 black keys.

F G A B

🎵 Alphabet Hunt

➤ How many FGAB groups can you find on your keyboard?

➤ Play all the FGAB groups from low to high.

➤ Circle the FGAB groups and write the letters on the keyboard below.

🎵 FGAB Family Members

Help find the missing family members of FGAB.

➤ Write the letter name under each key marked with an ✖.

Practice Plan

Your teacher will help you write your own **Practice Plan**.

➤ Practice
➤ Do flashcards
➤ Play Cuckoo
➤ Work on Rolls

Flying

LH   RH
4 3 2 1 ▲ 1 2 3 4
Middle C

Gliding

RH
F →
1 2 3 4 3 2 1   2 3 4 3 2 3

p Birds and planes and | clouds up high, | mov-ing in the | clear blue sky.

F →
LH

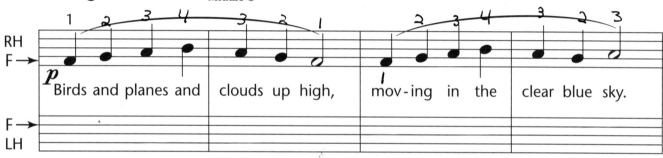

F →

Birds and planes and | clouds go by, | I wish I could | fly so high.

F →
4 3 2 1 2 3 4   4 3 2 3   4 3 4

You Be the Judge!

Did you hear:
• *p* sounds?
• legato phrases?

55-56   28

Student plays:

Teacher accompaniment

p con pedale

Practice Plan

➤ **T I =** _____

➤ Tap and say which hand plays (right or both).

➤ Which fingers play the LH part? Which LH measure is different?

➤ **P** = Phrases or patterns. Find and circle repeated patterns.

➤ Play and ta or sing the words.

FGAB Polka

LH / RH

3 2   1 2 3 4

Middle C

Fast

RH
F →   1   2   3   4   3   3   3   4   3   2   2   1   1   1

ƒ F   G   A   B,   turn a-round.   B   A   G   G,   pol - ka sound!

G →
LH
                     2
                     3   2
                                                         3

F →   1   2   3   4   3   3   3   4   3   2   2   1   1   1

F   G   A   B,   step and turn.   B   A   G   G,   now you've learned!

G →
                     2
                     3   2

57-58   29

Student plays:

Teacher accompaniment

9:4

mƒ

1.   2.

CELEBRATE PIANO!™ LEVEL 1A   **59**

3rds skip
- from a line to the next line
- from a space to the next space
- a letter name
- a finger

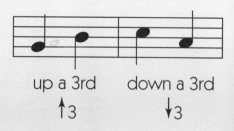

up a 3rd   down a 3rd
↑3   ↓3

Discovering 3rds

On the staff, 3rds skip a line or space.

➤ Draw an ✖ on the skipped line or space between the 3rds. Label the 3rds going up or down.

↑3   ↓3   ↓3   ↑3   ↓3   ↓3

On the white keys, 3rds skip a white key or letter name.

➤ Draw a ✔ on the key a 3rd above the given key. Draw an ✖ on the skipped key. Play these 3rds.

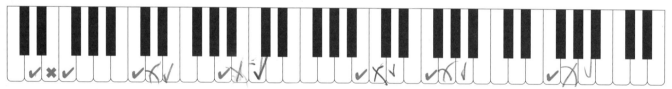

In your hand, 3rds skip a finger.

➤ Name the finger number for skipping up or down a 3rd.

LH:
finger 1, ↓3 is finger _____3_____
finger 2, ↓3 is finger _____4_____
finger 3, ↓3 is finger _____5_____

RH:
finger 1, ↑3 is finger _____3_____
finger 2, ↑3 is finger _____4_____
finger 3, ↑3 is finger _____5_____

Practice Plan

➤ **TIP** = _____

➤ Say the finger numbers as you play on the keyboard cover.

➤ **PS** = Play and say intervals, ta's, note names, or words.

Trombones

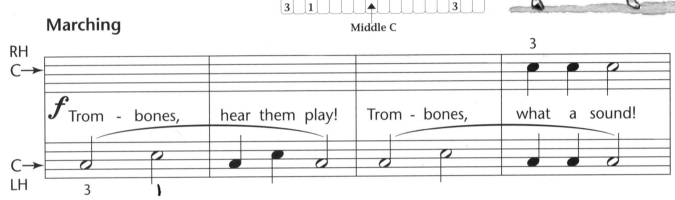

Marching

LH · · · Middle C · · · RH
3 1   3

RH
C→

f Trom - bones, | hear them play! | Trom - bones, | what a sound!
3   1

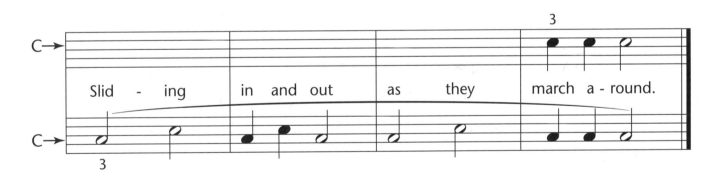

C→

Slid - ing | in and out | as they | march a - round.
3

You Be the Judge!

Did you hear:
• *f* sounds?
• legato phrases?
• a steady beat?

Teacher accompaniment. Student plays as written.

59-60 30   𝄢 4/4 ...
f

Practice Plan

➤ **T I P** = _____

➤ Say the finger numbers as you play on the keyboard cover.

➤ Circle the repeat sign.

➤ **PS** = Play and say intervals, ta's, note names, or words.

Repeat Sign

A repeat sign tells you to go back to the beginning and play again.

Fuzzy Caterpillar

Creeping

Transpose

Play **Fuzzy Caterpillar** starting on F or C.

Student plays:

Teacher accompaniment

61-62   31

Legato Warm-up

F F5

➤ Tap and ta the example.

➤ Sing the finger numbers as you play on the keyboard cover.

➤ Play legato with firm, rounded fingers.

➤ Remember to end the phrase softly.

Melodic and Harmonic 3rds

Melodic 3rd: A melodic 3rd has single notes played one at a time.

Harmonic 3rd: A harmonic 3rd has two notes played together.

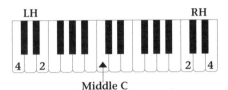

Interval Safari: Cuckoo Bird Song ^

The **Cuckoo Bird Song** uses 3rds.

➤ Sing and play the **Cuckoo Bird Song**. Start on Middle C with RH finger 1.

Cuck-oo bird,   Cuck-oo bird,   Can you hear the   cuck-oo bird?

➤ Sing this new song at least twice a day. Play Middle C and E (up a 3rd) to check that you are singing in tune.

^combining 2nds and 3rds

📖 Word Search

➤ Fill in the missing letters in the alphabet chains.

➤ Write those letters in the blanks to the right to discover the hidden word.

➤ Play the word on the keyboard.

1. A **B** C D _E_ F _G_ = **B** E G

2. G _A_ B _C_ D _E_ F = A C E

3. _F_ G _A_ B _C_ D _E_ = F A C E

4. _C_ D E F G _A_ _B_ = C A B

🥁 Tapping Game

➤ Tap and ta these rhythm lines using RH, LH, and hands together.

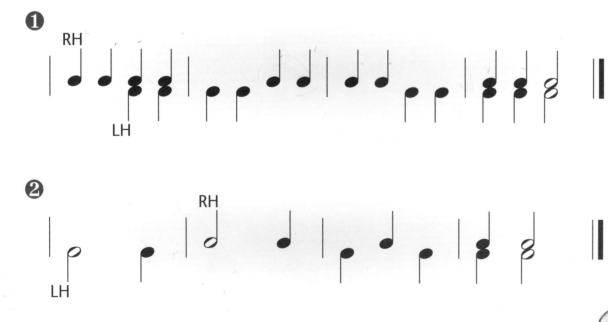

🎧 Pattern Detective

Listen as your teacher plays one of the rhythmic patterns in each example.

➤ Point to the pattern your teacher plays.

➤ Play each pattern yourself.

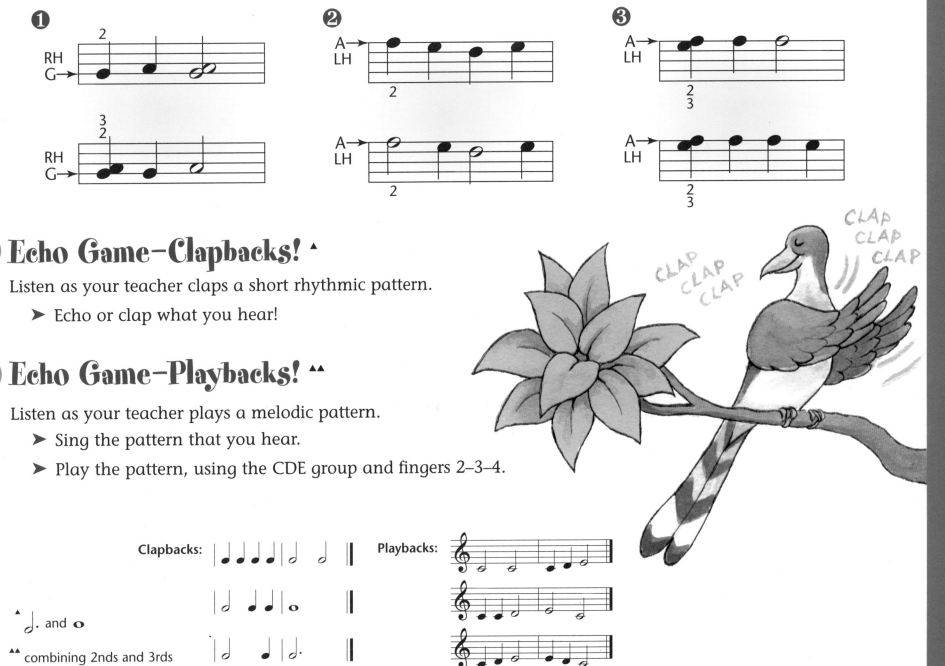

🎧 Echo Game—Clapbacks! ▲

Listen as your teacher claps a short rhythmic pattern.

➤ Echo or clap what you hear!

🎧 Echo Game—Playbacks! ▲▲

Listen as your teacher plays a melodic pattern.

➤ Sing the pattern that you hear.

➤ Play the pattern, using the CDE group and fingers 2–3–4.

🎼 Dancing Letters

Make up your own CDE or FGAB song titled **Dancing Letters**.

➤ Choose from: *p* and *f*

♩ and ♪

legato

2nds or 3rds

➤ Draw your song.

Practice Plan

➤ **TIP** = _Tap, interval, phrases_

➤ Say the RH finger numbers as you play on the keyboard cover.

➤ Name the first note in measure 5.

➤ Circle the harmonic 3rds.

➤ **PS** = Play and say intervals, ta's, or note names.

Cuckoo Bird Concert

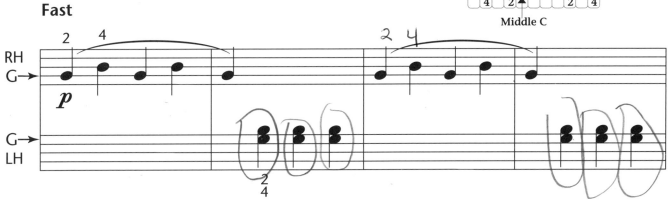

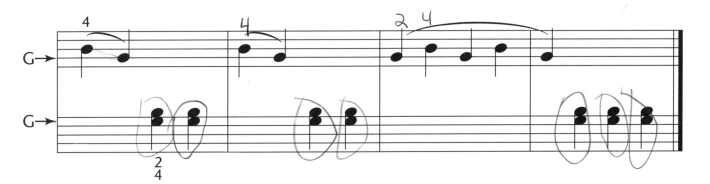

Transpose

Play **Cuckoo Bird Concert** in this new position:

Student plays:

Teacher accompaniment

Finger Warm-ups

F6

➤ Write the interval direction and size. Did you find both 2nds and 3rds?

➤ Say the finger numbers as you play on the keyboard cover.

➤ Play and ta. Remember to play legato and end each phrase softly.

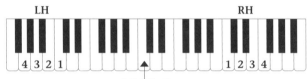

LH   RH

4 3 2 1   1 2 3 4

Middle C

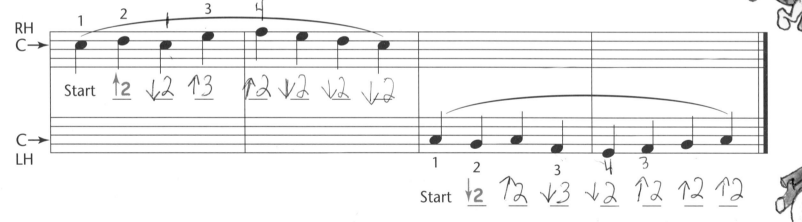

RH
C→

1   2   3   4

Start ↑2 ↓2 ↑3   ↑2 ↓2 ↓2 ↓2

C→
LH

                              1   2   3   4   3

Start ↓2 ↑2 ↓3 ↓2 ↑2 ↑2 ↑2

Interval Safari

➤ Sing the **Middle C Song**.

➤ Sing the **Busy Bee Song** (2nds). *Page 36*

➤ Sing the **Cuckoo Bird Song** (3rds). Play Middle C and E *— Page 63*
(up a 3rd) to check that you are singing in tune.   *Page 27*

Teacher: Have your student identify harmonic and melodic 2nds and 3rds.

Practice Plan

➤ **T I P** = ~~tap / interval / phrase~~

➤ What is the dynamic marking? *f* = loud

➤ Circle the 3rds.

➤ **PS** = Play and say intervals, ta's, note names, or words.

Toy Soldier March

Steady march

LH   RH

4 3 2 1   1 2 3 4

Middle C

f See them march-ing two by two, un-i-forms of red and blue.

Guard-ing all the oth-er toys, keep them safe for girls and boys.

69-70   35

Student plays:

Teacher accompaniment

simile

mp

Dotted Half Note 𝅗𝅥. = ta-ah-ah		Whole Note o = ta-ah-ah-ah
𝅗𝅥. = 3 beats		o = 4 beats
𝅗𝅥. = 𝅘𝅥 𝅘𝅥 𝅘𝅥		o = 𝅘𝅥 𝅘𝅥 𝅘𝅥 𝅘𝅥

(F) Rockin' Rhythms

F7

➤ Clap and ta these rhythmic patterns:

❶

ta   ta   ta   ta - ah - ah   ta   ta   ta   ta - ah - ah

❷

ta   ta   ta   ta   ta - ah - ah - ah   ta - ah   ta - ah   ta - ah - ah - ah

Tapping Rhythms

➤ Tap and say which hand plays (left, right, or both).

❶
RH

LH

❷ RH

LH

❸ Choose one of the rhythmic patterns and use it to make up your own piece. You might call it **Rhythm Machine** or **Robots!**

Practice Plan

➤ **T I P** = <u>tap / interval / phrase (4)</u>

➤ Name the first note in measure 7. G♩

➤ What are the dynamics in this piece? Soft ➝ loud

➤ **PS** = Play and say intervals, ta's, note names, or words.

My New Bike

LH   RH
3 2 1 ▲   1 2 3
Middle C

Coasting along

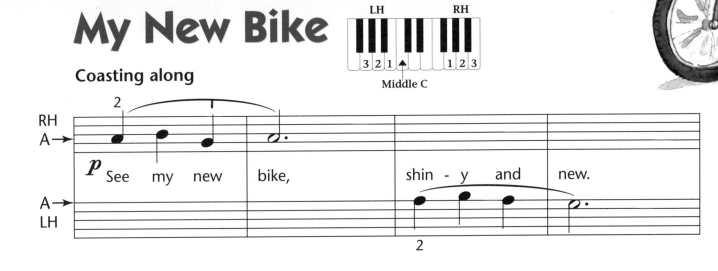

RH
A →
p See   my   new   bike,   shin - y   and   new.

A →
LH

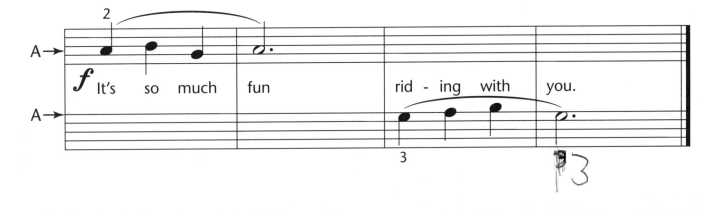

A →
f It's   so   much   fun   rid - ing   with   you.

A →

Transpose

Play **My New Bike** in this new position:

LH   RH
3 2 1   1 2 3

▲
Middle C

🖸 💾

71-72 36

Student plays:

Teacher accompaniment

Practice Plan

➤ **TIP** = _tap interval phrase_

➤ Circle the measures where you play hands together.

➤ In which measure does the LH play the melody? What is the starting note?

➤ **PS** = Play and say intervals, ta's, note names, or words.

Whole-note Cheer

With spirit

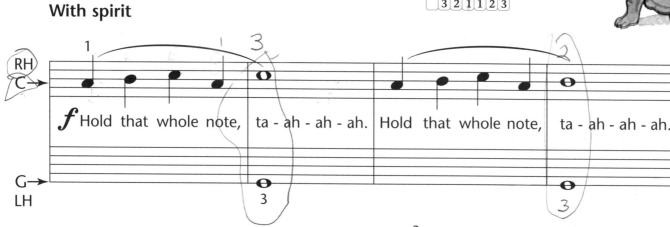

f Hold that whole note, ta - ah - ah - ah. Hold that whole note, ta - ah - ah - ah.

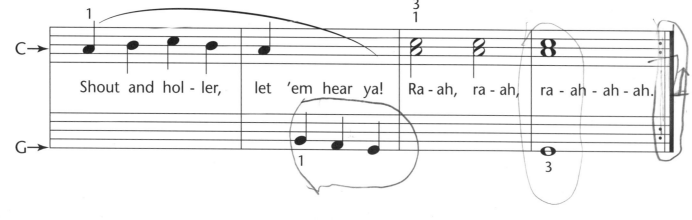

Shout and hol - ler, let 'em hear ya! Ra - ah, ra - ah, ra - ah - ah - ah.

You Be the Judge!

Did you hear:
- *f* ?
- phrases?
- legato?

73-74   37   Student plays: Teacher accompaniment

Practice Plan

➤ **T** = tap
➤ **I** = interval
➤ **P** = phrase
➤ **PS** = Play/Say

Old MacDonald

Middle C

LH   RH
3 2   2 3 4

Folk song

f Old Mac-Don-ald | had a farm, | e - i - e - i - o. | And

on his farm he | had some pigs, | e - i - e - i - o.

Can you play the rest of this piece by ear?

Transpose

Play **Old MacDonald** in this new position:

LH   RH
3   2
2   3 4

75-76 38

Student plays:

Teacher accompaniment

mf

CELEBRATE PIANO!™ LEVEL 1A   73

Interval Dance ▴

LH   RH

Middle C

➤ Circle the harmonic 3rds. 4
➤ Play and ta.
➤ Play the quarter notes using short, detached sounds.

Word Search

➤ Find the hidden words by following the interval directions.
➤ Write the note names in the blanks to discover the hidden word. Play the words.

❶ B ↓2 ↓2 = B __A__ __G__

❷ E ↑3 same = E __G__ __G__

❸ C ↓3 ↑2 = C __A__ __B__

❹ G ↑2 ↑2 = G __A__ __B__

❺ A ↑3 ↑3 = A __C__ __E__

❻ F ↑3 ↑3 ↑3 = F __A__ __C__ __E__

❼ C ↓3 ↓2 ↓3 = C __A__ __G__ __E__

❽ D ↑2 same ↓2 = D __E__ __E__ __D__

Tic-Tac-Toe

➤ Put a ✔ on all the A's, an ✖ on all the C's, and an O on all the E's.

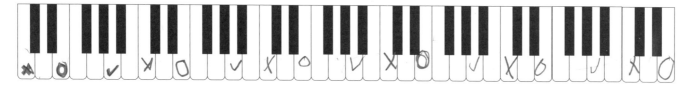

▴ staccato

Rhythm Maze

Can you help Cuckoo Bird find the way home?

➤ Follow the path by drawing a line connecting the groups of notes with 3 beats.

➤ Tap the rhythms along the path.

START

FINISH

👂 Listening Game

Listen as your teacher plays a 2nd up or down. Sing both notes of the interval.

➤ The first note is written for you. Write the other note that you hear.
Remember that 2nds go from a space to a line, or a line to a space.

👂 Echo Game–Clapbacks!

Listen as your teacher claps a short rhythmic pattern.

➤ Echo or clap what you hear!

👂 Echo Game–Playbacks!

Listen as your teacher plays a melodic pattern.

➤ Sing the pattern that you hear.

➤ Play the pattern, using the FGAB group.

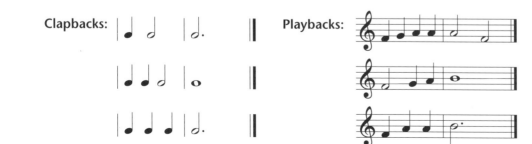

Pattern Detective

Listen as your teacher plays one of the patterns in each example.

➤ Circle the pattern your teacher plays.

➤ Practice reading and playing these patterns yourself!

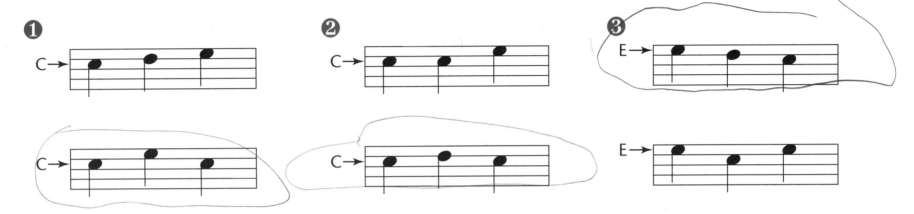

① C →

C → *(circled)*

② C →

C → *(circled)*

③ E → *(circled)*

E →

Question and Answer

Listen as your teacher plays a two-measure phrase (Question) using the CDE group.

➤ Echo the Question.

➤ Listen to the Question again.

➤ Make up and play a two-measure phrase (Answer) that ends on C. Be sure to ta.

Questions:

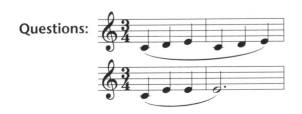

Practice Plan

Write your own **Practice Plan**.

➤ tap & ta
➤ f or p, line or space?
➤ clap
➤ which hand? 4 phases

The Echo Song

nwod ← | LH ... RH | → uP

3 2 1 ▲ 1 2 3 4
Middle C

Not too fast

RH
G→
3   1

3 4 3 3 1

f Ech - o...   *Ech - o...*   *f* I hear an ech - o

G→
LH

p

1   3

G→

p Talk - ing to my un - seen com - pan - ion.

G→
2

SKIP R 3

up zame down

5 lines
4 spaces

Student plays: Teacher accompaniment

77-78   39

mf con pedale *p*   *mf*   *p*

Congratulations!

Julianne Kalec

You have completed **Celebrate Piano!**™ Level 1A
and are now ready for **Celebrate Piano!**™ Level 1B.

Cathy Albergo   **J. Mitzi Kolar**   **Mark Mrozinski**

Caryl Palmer   4/27/05

Teacher   Date